AN
EASY-READ
FACT
BOOK

Prehistoric Mammals

Derek Hall

Franklin Watts

London   New York   Toronto   Sydney

© 1984 Franklin Watts Ltd

First published in Great Britain
   1984 by
Franklin Watts Ltd
12a Golden Square
London W1

First published in the USA by
Franklin Watts Inc.
387 Park Avenue South
New York
N.Y. 10016

UK ISBN: 0 86313 078 X
US ISBN 0-531-04707-5
Library of Congress Catalog Card
   Number: 83-50593

Designed by
Peter Luff

Edited by
Judith Maxwell

Illustrated by
Mike Atkinson
Robert and Rhoda Burns
Elizabeth Graham-Yooll
Michael Welply

Photographs supplied by
David Bayliss RIDA

Technical consultant
Dr Richard Moody

Printed in Great Britain by
   Cambus Litho, East Kilbride

AN EASY-READ FACT BOOK

Prehistoric Mammals

Contents

The first mammals

Mammals are intelligent, active animals. They usually have hair on their bodies to help them keep warm. Most mammals give birth to living young. The young are fed with milk from their mother's body. Cats, dogs, elephants, bats, mice and horses are all mammals. We are mammals too.

Prehistoric mammals are mammals that lived a long time ago, before recorded history.

The first mammals appeared on the Earth about 200 million years ago. Their ancestors were reptiles. But the mammals looked very different from reptiles. The first mammals were small, furry, shrew-like creatures. They probably hid among the plants for much of the day. They would only have scurried about to feed when it was dark. For at that time a group of reptiles – the dinosaurs – ruled the Earth.

▷This is a scene during the Triassic Period, about 200 million years ago. Some of the dinosaurs which roamed the Earth are shown in the background.
The small, shy mammals, like *Morganucodon*, probably ate insects, seeds and birds' eggs. *Cynognathus* was one of the mammals' ancestors.

4

Cynognathus

Morganucodon

The rise of mammals

△ *Taeniolabis* had gnawing teeth like rats and mice. It probably fed on bark, nuts and seeds.

The dinosaurs roamed the Earth for nearly 135 million years. Some were quite small, no bigger than a chicken. Others grew to be the biggest and fiercest animals living at that time. For example, *Tyrannosaurus* was over 20 ft (6 m) tall.

Then, quite suddenly, all the dinosaurs vanished. But other reptiles and the birds and mammals survived. No one is sure what caused the dinosaurs to die. This is one of nature's greatest mysteries.

With the dinosaurs gone, the Age of Mammals began. The mammals no longer had to hide away. They could eat the foods and live in the places left by the dinosaurs. These pictures show some of the different mammals that appeared. Most were bigger than the first mammals, and some were giants.

The Age of Mammals has lasted for 65 million years and is still continuing.

▷*Borhyaena* was a wolf-like, meat-eating mammal. It lived in South America during the Miocene Period. Meat-eating mammals ate other mammals, as well as birds and lizards.

▽These mammals ate plants. *Phenacodus* (right) was about the size of a sheep. It was an ancestor of the horse. *Uintatherium* (above) was much bigger, about the size of a rhinoceros.

The mammal family tree

Monotremes

This picture shows the many different sorts of mammals that have lived during the Age of Mammals. It also shows how they are related to each other. This is why it is called a family tree.

You can see from the family tree that most of the mammals living now are called placental mammals. Young placental mammals grow inside their mother's body until they are ready to be born. During this time, they are fed through a placenta. We are placental mammals.

Some groups became extinct

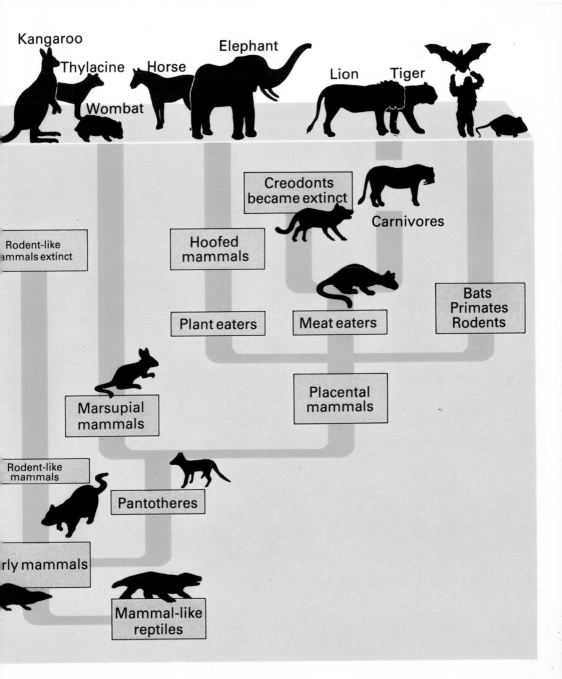

Kangaroo
Thylacine Horse Elephant
Wombat Lion Tiger

Creodonts became extinct
Carnivores

Rodent-like mammals extinct

Hoofed mammals

Bats Primates Rodents

Plant eaters Meat eaters

Marsupial mammals

Placental mammals

Rodent-like mammals

Pantotheres

Early mammals

Mammal-like reptiles

Why the mammals flourished

Mammals differ in many ways from the dinosaurs they replaced. These differences made them better suited to living on the Earth.

Mammals are cleverer than other animals. They can think up new ways to find food and to escape from danger.

△Among the cleverest animals is a group of mammals called primates. This is *Necrolemur*, one of the first primates.

▷Some mammals, such as the kangaroo shown here, carry their young even *after* they are born. If danger threatens, the baby kangaroo can jump back into its mother's pouch. Mammals with pouches are called marsupial mammals.

When the weather is very cold, a reptile slows down and cannot catch its food. It needs the Sun's rays to keep it warm. A mammal keeps its own body warm. So, when the weather changes, mammals can still move around to find food.

Most reptiles lay eggs. The eggs may be eaten by other animals. Most mammal mothers carry their young inside their bodies until they are born. This keeps the young safe and warm.

▽Wolves eat other animals. They can chase their prey over very long distances without tiring. Some animals were too big and powerful for a wolf to kill on its own. So wolves learned to hunt in packs, sharing their kill.

Mammals on the move

△ Reptiles living today, like this lizard, have arms and legs which jut out from the sides of their bodies. Because of this they cannot run as well as mammals.

The first mammals walked on all four legs, just as many of the reptiles did. But they could run faster than the reptiles. Most mammals still run on all fours – dogs and mice, for example.

Later, some mammals appeared which learned to fly. This meant that they could eat other flying animals, such as insects. Flying also gave them a new way to escape from danger. The first bats – the only flying mammals – appeared on Earth about 65 million years ago.

Other mammals left the land and started living in the water. About 40 million years ago, the 66 ft (20 m) long whale *Basilosaurus* swam in the seas. Other mammals, such as seals and hippopotamuses, spend part of their life in the water, and part on land.

Some mammals started to walk upright on only two legs. These were our ancestors.

△ A bat's wing is a piece of naked skin, stretched between its very long fingers and arms, and its legs.

△ *Mesohippus* is an ancestor of the horse. It had long legs, and could probably run quite fast to escape its enemies.

▷ The fierce-looking *Basilosaurus* was one of the first whales. All mammals breathe air. So whales must come to the surface of the water to breathe. Whales swim by lashing their powerful tails up and down.

13

Forgotten mammals

Millions of years ago, all the continents were joined together in one huge piece of land called Pangaea. Animals could roam anywhere they chose, for no seas separated the land.

During the Jurassic Period, Pangaea began to split up. The only mammals living in one part of Pangaea were monotremes (egg-laying mammals) and marsupials (pouched mammals). This part split off to become Australia.

Monotremes and marsupials died out over most of the world – killed by the placental mammals. But Australia was separated from the rest of the world by huge oceans. So here, these mammals were safe.

They flourished for millions of years, cut off from the rest of the world. Then people crossed the oceans in boats and found these forgotten mammals. Many of them still survive today.

▽ The globe below shows how the Earth looked when there was just one huge land, Pangaea.
  The globe on the right shows how the Earth looked after the continents separated.

Pangaea

▷ These two moles developed thousands of miles apart, yet they are remarkably similar.

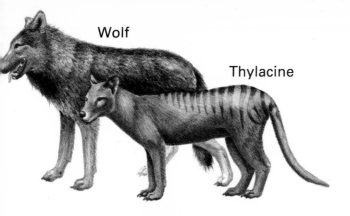

Wolf

Thylacine

◁The wolf is a placental mammal. It used to live in many parts of the world, but it never reached Australia. The marsupial thylacine is found in Tasmania, an island south of Australia. It lives in a similar way to the wolf. It is often called the Tasmanian wolf.

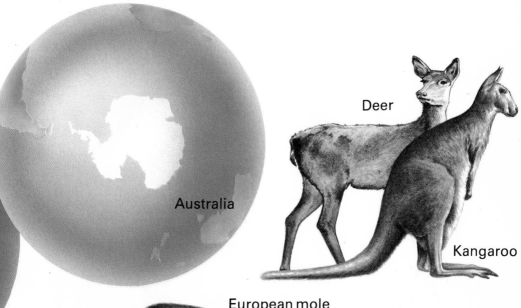

Australia

Deer

Kangaroo

European mole

Australian marsupial mole

△There are no deer in Australia. Instead, Australia has the kangaroo. Deer and kangaroos live in a very similar way. Both live in herds, and feed by grazing on plains and in forests.

15

Plant eaters

▽This great plant eater, *Brontotherium*, lived between 38 and 26 million years ago. It grew to about 15 ft (4.5 m) long. It had a huge double horn on its nose, and legs as thick as tree trunks.

In prehistoric times there were many plant-eating mammals, just as there are today. Their teeth were specially suited for eating plants. Some could only chew soft plants. They died out when the tough grasses began to grow instead.

▷This curious-looking mammal, *Glyptodon*, lived in South America. It was nearly 10 ft (3 m) long. A bony shell covered its head, body and tail. This protected it like a suit of armor.

The plant eaters were in danger of being killed by the meat-eating mammals. Many developed long legs to escape from their enemies. Some were protected by a tough skin. Others were safe just because they grew so big.

Some prehistoric plant eaters, such as the ancestors of horses and elephants, looked like some of the mammals we see today. Others looked very strange, and have long since become extinct.

▽ *Macrauchenia* looked rather like a cross between a camel and an elephant. It was about the same size and shape as a camel, but had a short trunk as well.

▽ *Pliohippus* was 6.5 ft (2 m) long.

17

Meat eaters

Many meat-eating mammals have lived during the past 65 million years. Some were quite small and ate only tiny animals such as insects. Many were big enough to kill the plant eaters which roamed the swamps and forests. Some were huge, ferocious beasts.

Many meat eaters had powerful teeth which could stab into and slice meat. Some also had sharp claws to help them catch their prey.

Many early meat eaters belonged to a group called the creodonts. These died out and were replaced by the carnivores. The carnivores included the saber-toothed cats and wolves. Saber-toothed cats were so called because they had two huge, sharp, curved teeth like sabers. The carnivores learned many different ways to catch their prey. The cats, dogs and bears living today are carnivores.

△ This saber-toothed cat probably tried to stay out of sight, hidden among the plants. It would then have surprised the rhinoceros by rushing out at it. With its fearsome teeth, it could quickly stab through the thick hide. Once the saber-toothed cat had had eaten its fill, the wolves would have come to eat the rest of the carcass.

Giant mammals

△ This picture shows the prehistoric *Baluchitherium* with an animal which we today think of as huge, the elephant. *Baluchitherium* could eat the leaves of trees far above the reach of other animals.

Most of us have seen large mammals, such as elephants and giraffes, at the zoo. Suppose, however, you suddenly saw cages containing armadillos nearly 10 ft (3 m) long, and sloths the size of elephants! Such huge mammals once existed.

Giant platypuses and kangaroos, and beavers as big as small bears once roamed the Earth. There were even hedgehogs the size of foxes, pigs as large as cows, and long-necked rhinoceroses as big as elephants.

Most of these giant mammals lived during the last 38 million years. No one is sure why these huge forms appeared. Many of them roamed the Earth until only a few million years ago. So it is quite likely that they would have been hunted by early Man. One of the most recently extinct giant mammals was a huge deer. Its antlers alone measured 13 ft (4 m) from tip to tip.

▽ Here are two of the huge mammals which lived during prehistoric times.

Diprotodon looked like a huge bear. It lived in Australia and grew to a length of 11 ft (3.3 m). *Megatherium* was a giant ground sloth, which lived in America. It was up to 20 ft (6 m) long and would have weighed several tons.

Megatherium

Diprotodon

Time stands still

When they died, most prehistoric mammals would have been eaten by other animals or just rotted away. So they would have left no trace. But some dead mammals were covered with sand or mud. The sand or mud slowly hardened into rock with the animal's remains locked away inside. The remains of animals or plants preserved in rocks are known as fossils.

▽ To become fossils, bones must be covered very quickly by sand or mud.

After millions of years, the bones are buried deep inside the Earth.

Today, scientists carefully dig them out and study them.

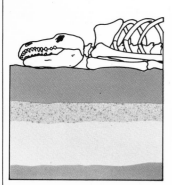

Scientists have found out about pre-historic mammals by studying their fossils. Teeth can show what sort of food an animal ate. From the leg bones, scientists may be able to tell whether the animal ran fast or crawled slowly. In this way, they can work out what the animal looked like and how it lived.

▽ This scene shows the Rancho La Brea tar pits, in California, in prehistoric times. The mammoth came to drink at the pool. Under the water was deep, sticky tar, and the mammoth sank into it and died. But the tar stopped its body from rotting. Fossils of mammoths, saber-toothed cats, wolves and many other animals have been found at Rancho La Brea.

Close-up on evolution

▽ The main changes in the evolution of the horse. *Hyracotherium* lived in swamps during the Eocene Period. Slowly the land became drier. *Miohippus* and *Merychippus* evolved. They were more suited to living on drier land.

All of today's mammals are descended from prehistoric mammals. Conditions on Earth slowly changed. The mammals slowly changed, or evolved, too. The new mammals were better suited to the new conditions. For example, a larger plant eater may have evolved to eat taller plants.

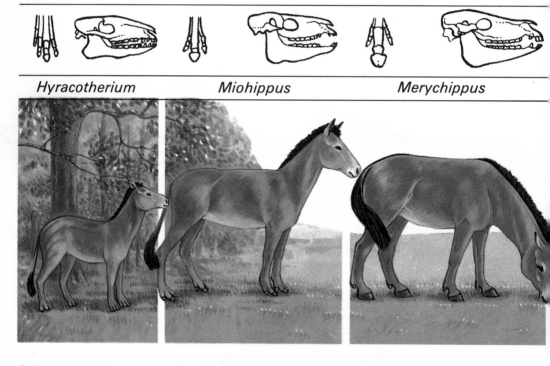

Hyracotherium   *Miohippus*   *Merychippus*

All the mammals around us have come about through this slow change or evolution. Most of their ancestors died out. But their remains may be preserved as fossils.

A great many fossils of the horse have been found. From these, scientists can trace the evolution of the horse over the last 50 million years. It slowly changed from a dog-sized creature living in swampy forests to the large hoofed animal which grazes on the plains today.

▽ Over millions of years, the great plains were formed. *Pliohippus* and the modern horse *Equus* grazed on these.

The pictures of the skulls show how the shape of their teeth changed. Their food changed from lush, swampy plants to tough grass. So, their teeth had to change too. The shape of the feet changed from toes to hoofs.

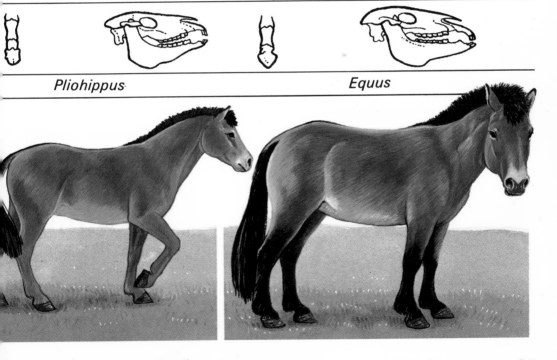

Pliohippus

Equus

The Ice Ages

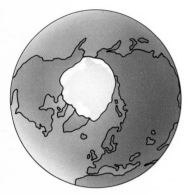

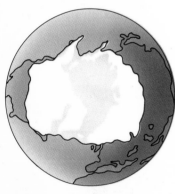

△ The globe at the top shows how much ice there is around the North Pole today. The globe above shows the extent of ice during the last Ice Age. Large parts of North America and Europe were covered in thick ice.

The Earth has become very cold several times during its history. These times are known as Ice Ages. During the Ice Ages, thick sheets of ice spread down from the poles to cover forests and plains. Ice Ages have occurred during the last 2 million years. During them, many of the mammals moved south. Here it was warmer and there was more food to eat.

Others were able to live in the colder north. Some made their homes in caves. Some grew thick, woolly coats. The woolly rhinoceroses and the woolly mammoths were kept warm by their thick coats. The woolly mammoth used its huge, curved tusks to clear away snow to find food.

Early Man lived during the recent Ice Ages. He hunted animals such as bears and woolly mammoths. He wore the skins of these animals and huddled around fires to keep warm.

▽This scene shows some of the mammals which lived during the Ice Ages. When the bear had caught its meal, it would have gone back to its warm cave. Woolly rhinoceroses, reindeer and woolly mammoths had to find what shelter they could on the open ground.

The Age of Man

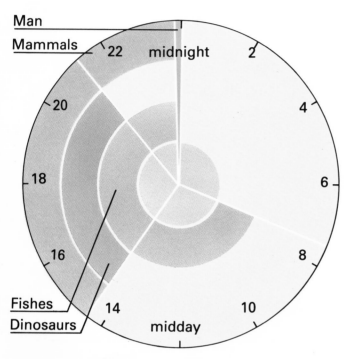

Man
Mammals
22 midnight 2
20
18 4
6
16 8
Fishes
Dinosaurs 14 10
midday

▷This ape-man is *Australopithecus*. It lived in Africa between 4 and 1 million years ago. Like us, it walked on two feet, but its brain was only about half the size of ours.

Scientists do not think that we evolved from this creature, but from other sorts of ape-men.

△This picture shows the last 570 million years as a 24-hour clock. From this, you can see how short a time Man has been on the Earth. On our clock, Man appears just before midnight! Compare this time with the appearance of the fishes, or the length of time that dinosaurs ruled the Earth.

We are mammals. We belong to a group of mammals called the primates. The first primates were small animals which lived in trees. Over millions of years many different sorts of primates evolved from these creatures. Some, such as monkeys, continued to live in the trees. Others, including our ancestors, started living on the ground.

The first ape that was like us in many ways was *Ramapithecus*. It lived in forests about 12 million years ago. Several kinds of ape-men then lived on the Earth. They walked on two legs instead of on all four. No one is sure which ones were our ancestors. Scientists think that modern Man first appeared 500,000 to 250,000 years ago.

8,839

Glossary

Here is a list of some of the technical words used in this book.

Carnivores
Meat-eating mammals which appeared towards the end of the Cretaceous Period. Many carnivores are living today, such as lions, wolves and bears.

Creodonts
Meat-eating mammals which lived from the Cretaceous Period to the Eocene Period.

Cretaceous Period
Period of the Earth's history from about 135 million to 65 million years ago.

Eocene Period
Period of the Earth's history from about 54 million to 38 million years ago.

Evolution
The process of slow change by which all the animals and plants around us have developed.

Extinct
This word is used to describe a group of animals or plants which no longer have any living members.

Fossils
The preserved remains of dead animals or plants.

Jurassic Period
Period of the Earth's history from about 195 million to 135 million years ago.

Marsupials
Mammals in which the young develop in a special pouch after being born. Most marsupials are found only in Australia. A few also live in S. America.

Miocene Period
Period of the Earth's history from about 26 million to 7 million years ago.

Monotremes
Mammals which lay eggs. They are found only in parts of Australasia.

Pangaea
The name given to the continents when they were all joined together.

Pantotheres
Group of early mammals from which marsupial and placental mammals evolved.

Primates
Group of mammals which includes the lorises, lemurs, monkeys, apes and Man.

Triassic Period
Period of the Earth's history from about 225 million to 195 million years ago.

Prehistoric mammal facts

Here are some interesting facts about prehistoric mammals.

The largest ever land mammal was a long-necked rhinoceros, called *Baluchitherium*. It stood 18 ft (5.5 m) at the shoulder, and had a head 4 ft (1.2 m) long.

The largest known mammals are not always extinct ones! The largest animal that has ever lived is the 100 ft (30 m) long blue whale.

During the last Ice Age some parts of the ice sheet were 2 miles (3 km) thick. So much of the Earth's water turned to ice that sea-levels were 330 ft (100 m) lower than they are today.

▷Scientists who work with fossils are called palaeontologists. They use special hammers and chisels to remove rocks containing fossils.

Elephas trogontheri, an early mammoth, stood 15 ft (4.5 m) at the shoulder. It was the largest elephant ever to have lived.

Homo sapiens, the species of Man to which we belong, has been on Earth for less than 500,000 years. The race of Man which includes ourselves (*Homo sapiens sapiens*) has lived on Earth for about 30,000 years.

Index